STEP-BY-STEP GARDEN PROJECTS

Peter McHoy

Stonework

How to create stone gardens and ornaments,
and build paths, patios, walls, steps and ponds

AURA

Step-by-Step Garden Projects
Stonework

Peter McHoy

Copyright © 1999
Aura Books

This edition published in 2000 by **Aura Books**

Produced by Transedition Limited, Oxford OX4 4DJ, England

Editing and layout: Asgard Publishing Services, Leeds

Typesetting: Organ Graphic, Abingdon

Picture credits

All photographs by the author. All drawings by Colin Fargher, Fargher Design, Douglas, Isle of Man.

10 9 8 7 6 5 4 3

Printed in Dubai

ISBN 1 901683 07 9

Peter McHoy has worked on six gardening magazines, three of them as editor, but now devotes most of his time to writing and photography. He has written about 50 books, most of them on gardening, and contributes regular garden features to *Park Home* and *Practical Householder*. He also runs his own horticultural photographic library.

His interest in gardening goes back to childhood — he can remember the excitement of looking over the hedge and being fascinated by a neighbour's greenhouse full of seedlings in spring. This early enthusiasm sparked a particular interest in seeds, and he became a seed analyst before a change of direction took him into publishing over 30 years ago.

He has always been interested in the role of rocks in the garden, and appreciates the diverse possibilities that rocks and stones offer for garden features of all kinds. He shares his enthusiasm and know-how with you in the following pages.

CONTENTS

4   **Introduction**
The beauty of rocks   5

8   **Tools and equipment**
Equipment you may need   8

10   **Materials**
Buying rock and stone   10
Stone for paving   11
Rockery stone   12
Walling stone   14

16   **Paths and patios**
Crazy-paving   16
Rectangular paving   20

24   **Raised beds**
Planning a raised bed   24
Mortared flints   25
Using slabs   26

28   **Garden walls**
Cutting and shaping stone   28
Boundary walls   30
Walls to plant in   32
Dry stone walls   34

38   **Retaining walls**
A retaining bank   38
A low retaining wall for a bed   40

42   **Steps**
Making steps   42
Steps with a difference   46

48   **Gravel and stone gardens**
Formal gravel gardens   48
Informal gravel gardens   52
Stone gardens   54

56   **Rock and water**
A rock cascade   56
Traditional rock banks   60
Island rock beds   64
A Mediterranean-style pond   66

70   **Special projects**
Miniature rock gardens   70
Moving and lifting rocks   71
Centres of attraction   72
Rock and water   73
Stepping stones   74
Strewing stones   75

76   **Glossary**
Useful information   76

80   **Index**

Natural stone harmonises so well with plants, and will give your garden a timeless appeal.

The beauty of rocks

Rock is a natural landscape material that has many roles to play in a well-designed garden. Indeed, almost every garden would benefit from a rock feature of some sort.

Most of us think first of the traditional rock garden, but then, if we don't have the space or a suitable site for a rock garden, we take the potential of rock no further. This will almost certainly mean missed opportunities — for example, a rock-bed set in the lawn can look very attractive and will provide an opportunity to grow alpines that may be difficult to integrate naturally into other parts of the garden. There are also lots of alpines (or rock plants if you prefer) that can be grown very successfully in stone walls. Indeed, this is the natural habitat for some of them.

Natural stone paving slabs are expensive and less readily available than the more popular concrete ones, yet real stone paving will give your garden that sense of maturity and class that concrete paving can seldom match. If you plan to use natural stone for your paving, then it's also worth trying to use the same material for your steps.

Be creative
Rocks and stones can be used to make an interesting low-maintenance garden. Gravel and crushed stone are both widely used for creating a hard landscaping surface. Gravel gardens can be planted with subjects that thrive in dry places, making a garden that is drought-resistant as well as low-maintenance (see picture overleaf).

If you want something a little more unusual, then you could consider a stone garden, where larger rocks and boulders are used for their

Large rocks can be used in a similar way to sculptures, to create striking focal points.

shape, form and texture, with just a few plants introduced for contrast and to soften the effect. A large boulder or a big and distinctive-looking rock can be used as a focal point, rather like an ornament, and one with a smooth, flat surface could perhaps make a natural-looking seat.

Other simple but superbly effective projects with rock include stepping-stones through a pond, across a stream or even across the lawn, and a drilled boulder coupled to a hidden pump and cleverly positioned above an unseen reservoir of water.

These are just some of the ways in which rock can be used in the garden, and most of these projects can be found within the following pages.

However, you should always bear in mind that rock is not a standard product like a manu-factured paving slab or walling block. You must always work with the material and modify the plans or instructions to suit what you're working with.

Apart from a dwarf conifer and a golden-green carpet of Sagina subulata *'Aurea', this garden is composed entirely of various types of rocks and stones, yet it certainly doesn't lack impact.*

Equipment you may need

If you're making a simple rock garden, or just using a boulder or stone as an ornament, then the tools you'll required are minimal — though you may be very glad of a crowbar to assist your muscle-power.

If you're building something more structural, such as a dry stone wall, or making a mortared raised bed, choosing the right tools will help to create a more professional finish as well as making the job easier.

These few basic tools are all you're likely to need for most stonework jobs (top to bottom, then left to right): **1** *spirit-level;* **2** *goggles;* **3** *string and pegs;* **4** *measuring tape;* **5** *bolster chisel;* **6** *stone hammer;* **7** *club hammer.*

Tools to buy

A **club hammer**, **cold chisels** and a **bolster chisel** (with a wider blade) are invaluable for cutting rocks to size. Even if you're making a rock garden where most rocks will be left untouched, you may need to break a few rocks to produce smaller pieces to fill a particular position.

Once you start hammering and chiselling, **goggles** and **gloves** become *essential* wear. Stone may fragment unpredictably, so protect your eyes and keep other people, especially children, beyond the range of flying splinters.

A pair of **shoes** or **boots** with reinforced toe-caps is highly desirable if you are moving large rocks, though I suspect few amateurs would bother to buy them.

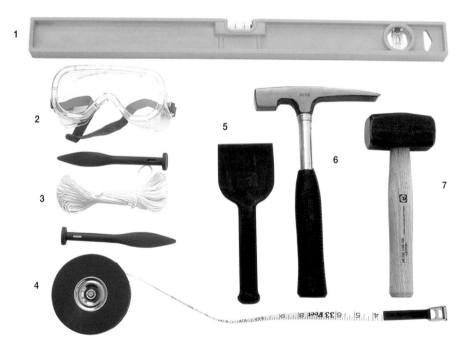

If you're laying walls of any kind, even if it's only to make a raised bed, you will need a long **measuring tape**, **string** and **pegs** to keep your construction on the straight and narrow. A long **spirit-level** will be useful for checking levels and verticals, though with something as irregular as stone a spirit-level can only be used as a guide.

If you're planning mortared walls, a **raking tool** to strike off the mortar neatly when the joints have been made could be useful, but a small **pointing trowel** is likely to be more effective with the irregular surfaces of most stone walling blocks.

A **stone hammer**, which has one flat face and one bevelled, is especially useful if you're building a stone wall. You can both split and shape rock with this useful tool. If you have much walling to do, consider buying two stone hammers: a heavy one and a light one (a geologist's hammer).

Tools to make

A **straight-edge** is useful for checking whether paving and walls are level; it is usually used to support a spirit-level. All you need is a straight-edged piece of wood about 8–10 ft (2.4–3 m) long, but it must have parallel sides and not be warped or distorted.

A **builder's square** is useful for establishing right-angles, and is easily made from a few lengths of scrap timber. You simply screw together three lengths of timber of appropriate size. It's the proportions that are important, rather than the absolute lengths: they must be exactly 3:4:5 (see illustration). When assembled it will form a 90° angle.

This simple builder's square is a tool for checking right-angles, and can be made from scrap wood.

Tools to hire

If you have to prepare concrete footings (foundations) for walls or paths, hiring a **concrete mixer** could save a lot of time and effort. A small electric mixer may be adequate if the job is not large. A hydraulic **block splitter** is usually used for concrete or clay paving, but it may also be useful for cutting stone paving to size. Alternatively, an **angle grinder** (disc cutter) can be used.

Crowbars are inexpensive to hire, and unless you require one for other jobs it's probably worth hiring one rather than purchasing a tool you may not use again. If heavy rocks have to be moved, perhaps to construct a rock garden, it's worth hiring a couple of them as you'll need an assistant to move large rocks.

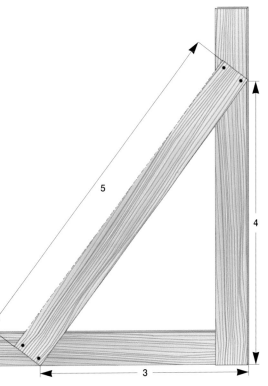

Buying rock and stone

Choosing and buying rock and stone is a more difficult task than it sounds. What's available at a reasonable price depends very much on where you live. Transporting rock over long distances can be expensive — and even then a granite rock might look out of place in a part of the countryside where sandstone is the underlying rock. Choosing a type of rock found locally is usually cheaper, and the chances are that it will blend in with the surrounding countryside better than a rock that does not 'belong'.

You can't simply order rocks or stone paving and be sure of what you'll receive, in the way you can with manufactured products. Ideally you need to see before you buy, and to select the particular pieces that you want.

Waterworn limestone is only available from certain areas of the country. This is such a desirable type of stone for a rock garden or watercourse that some gardeners are prepared to pay a high price and have it transported over long distances. However, the limestone pavements from which this rock is sometimes quarried form a unique natural geological structure and wildlife habitat, and so its use is to be discouraged. The exception is if you can obtain recycled waterworn limestone from an existing garden: old rockeries are sometimes dismantled and the rock sold.

The most sensible way to buy rock and stone for your garden is to go to a stone merchant, who should stock a wide range of different kinds at competitive prices. Look under 'Stone merchants' in trade directories such as the Yellow Pages, and go along to your local suppliers to see what's available.

You will also find some quarries from further afield advertising under 'Stone merchants', and for a large quantity or a special piece of rock it can be worth giving them a call.

Buying by weight

Rockery and paving stone is usually sold by weight. Many stone merchants will allow you to choose your own pieces, and may give you a pallet to put them on for weighing later.

Other merchants may be less precise, and quote you a price simply by casting an eye over a heap of rocks.

Deciding how much you need can be difficult, as an apparently large heap of rocks may not go as far as you think — bear in mind that much of the rock will be beneath the ground once in position in a rock garden. As a guide, a tonne of sandstone might contain about 30 pieces, with some of the large individual rocks weighing 1 cwt (50 kg).

Sometimes rock is sold by the cubic yard or metre. As a very rough guide, 1 cu yd of sandstone might be sufficient to make 5 sq yd of rockery (1 m^3 sufficient for 5.5 m^2). These are broad generalisations, however, so you should seek advice from the supplier.

Garden centres

Good garden centres usually stock a small range of stone suitable for a rockery, and sometimes there may be a small selection of stone suitable for paving. Certainly you should be able to obtain a selection of coloured gravels or crushed stone. These are likely to be sold in bags, however, which is often an expensive way to buy them.

Builders' merchants

The range of stone and gravel available from builders' merchants may be limited. On the other hand, they can often deliver a bulk quantity at reasonable cost.

Stone for paving

The range of stone suitable for paving is limited, and your choice will be influenced by availability and price. One of the best, and most expensive, is York stone, but others may be available locally. Slate makes a pleasing path, and you can sometimes obtain this from garden centres as well as stone merchants.

Don't expect paving stone to be an even thickness; you will probably have to adjust the depth of the bedding mortar to accommodate varying thicknesses.

York stone is the best material for paving, but it's expensive. Moreover, large pieces are heavy to work with, and cutting the slabs to shape can also be exacting work. (If York stone like this proves too much of a challenge, then slate is less expensive and easier to work with.)

Rockery stone

Finding suitable rockery stone is almost as difficult as positioning it. As a rule, it's best to choose a stone that occurs naturally in the region in which you live: it's more likely to blend in with the landscape, and it should be cheaper.

These are the types of rock you are most likely to find in the UK:

Chalk
Chalk is too soft to use for a rock garden — it will wear and weather too quickly.

Granite
This hard volcanic rock may be reddish, purple-brown, green or blue-grey. As it's an acidic rock, it's useful for growing lime-hating plants such as heathers. On the other hand, the pieces are usually very angular, which makes them difficult to place convincingly, and they can look stark because they weather slowly.

Limestone
Limestone, formed from the shell remains of minute sea creatures, makes a pleasing rock garden. Most limestones are whitish or grey, but some may be pale cream, bluish or buff-coloured, depending on their source. They have different characteristics too, some splitting more easily that others into thin flagstones.

All rocks will change colour and mellow as they weather, but this applies especially to limestone.

Sandstone
This relatively soft stone often has more rounded surfaces than the harder rocks. It also generally lacks those attractive strata marks that are a feature of some other rocks. The usual colour is brown, but it may be tinged with green or purple.

Weathered limestone is full of character and much sought after for rock gardens. However, waterworn limestone is not advisable unless recycled from a dismantled rock garden, because its continued exploitation threatens the valuable habitats from which it is quarried.

Slate

This rock isn't used much for rock gardens or walls. But because it splits into layers easily, it's sometimes used for paving. Another popular use is for watercourses and cascades which have rocks as a feature. Colours include blue-grey, green and purplish.

Tufa

Although seldom used for a complete rock garden, this pumice-like rock (a form of limestone) is often used to decorate sink gardens, or to make small rock features where alpines are inserted directly into the rock: it's soft enough to be drilled to make planting holes. When freshly quarried, it's buff-coloured and sometimes almost dazzling white in strong sunshine, but it soon mellows to grey.

The structure is full of holes, making it a very porous rock. This also makes it a light rock for a given size, so if buying by weight, it's best to make your purchase when the rock's dry, rather than when it's heavy from absorbed moisture!

Walling stone

Most of the rocks already described can be used for walls, but you'll find a variety of local stones available too. Using a local stone for a garden wall can be even more important than for a rock garden. A Sussex flint wall, for example, would probably look out of place among the traditional limestone walls of the Cotswolds; a slate wall might look quite incongruous among the millstone grit of the Pennines.

Whatever type of walling stone is available locally, you will probably have the option of buying it either as random stone or as dressed (squared-off) stone.

Random stone

When sold for walling, random stones are usually fairly flat on the top and bottom, but the dimensions are variable. By choosing stones of similar size, you can create an informal effect, but with clear courses running in horizontal lines. If you choose random stones in a variety of sizes, on the other hand, the effect is more like that of vertical crazy-paving. For stability, random blocks of very different sizes are best mortared together; dry stone walling (see pages 34–37) is a challenging project for a beginner.

Dressed stone

These stones are more like manufactured walling blocks, though they are less regular in size. They are hand-made with a fairly uniform width and height, usually with a decorative outer face or faces. The best way to choose what's appropriate is to visit a quarry or stone merchant and see for yourself.

This stone wall is to be found at Iford Manor in Gloucestershire. One this height is an ambitious project for an amateur, but a more modest one will still give your garden lots of appeal.

Crazy-paving

Natural stone crazy-paving is aesthetically much more pleasing than the broken concrete paving slabs sometimes used. Your stone merchant or garden centre should be able to supply thin-cut stone suitable for the job, though because of the irregular shape of the paving stones it can be difficult to estimate exactly how much you will require.

Crazy-paving is made from pieces of broken slabs, laid in such as way that they produce a random but decorative pattern. It needs careful thought to produce a strong path with a reasonably symmetrical appearance.

Before you start laying the stone, make some attempt to grade the pieces according to size, as it's a good idea to use mainly large pieces along the edge of the paved area, especially if it's a path. You'll also find it easier to choose an appropriate piece as you work than if you leave all the stone unsorted in one large heap.

The stone is likely to arrive on a pallet, and if you have several pallets it may be impractical to lay out all the pieces to grade them first. In that case, simply work with a small amount at a time, grading that and laying some of the paving before moving on to the next batch. This will also ensure that you don't use all the biggest and best pieces of stone first, leaving all the smaller bits to use up at the end.

A firm footing

The path shown on page 18 was laid over existing paving slabs, just to improve the appearance, but if you're starting with bare ground, prepare a concrete base first.

Lay out an area of paving 'dry', positioning just the main pieces. It's wise to use large pieces at the edge for stability. This is especially important with a path, and if the paving is slightly higher than the adjoining bed or at the edge of a pond. For a path, try to arrange large pieces with one relatively straight side at the edge.

Once the edge pieces of a path have been positioned loosely, choose more large pieces for the centre of the path. Those without a good straight edge can be used for these. Use the smaller pieces to fill in between the larger ones.

Once you're happy with the provisional positioning, mortar the stones into position. If the stones are very uneven in thickness, you may have to make the mortar bed fairly deep to accommodate the thickest stones; otherwise try splitting any that are too thick.

Press the stones into the bed of mortar, then use a spirit-level to check that the surface is reasonably level. If you are paving a large area, it's sensible to have a gentle slope in one direction so that rainwater runs off freely.

Cutting and trimming

For more tips on how to cut and shape paving stones to suit your own particular requirements, turn to page 19 overleaf.

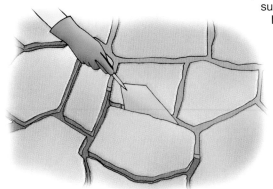

Wipe off any mortar that you get on the exposed surface of the stones before it dries, then leave the mortar to set before pointing.

Once the mortar has set firm enough for the paving to be walked on, mortar the joints for a neat finish. A small pointing trowel is ideal for this job, making it easy to strike the mortar off flush with the surface or just a little below, according to preference.

If you're using a dark stone such as slate, pale mortar joints may look a little too dominant. If you want a darker joint, add a colouring powder to the mortar when you mix it.

Removing a bump

Sometimes a stone won't fit because of a bump or lump that makes it too deep. It's worth trying to remove the bump rather than discarding the stone as unsuitable.

Try using a cold chisel to chip a thin score-line all around the lump, then use the chisel with its blade as flat as possible against the main surface to break it off. Alternatively, try using a stone hammer.

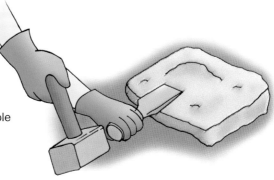

Trimming an edge

Draw a line where you want to trim the stone, or scribe it with a cold chisel. Use a bolster chisel and club hammer to score all around the stone, gradually deepening the score-line. It should eventually break fairly smoothly if hit firmly with a club hammer and bolster chisel.

If you have a stone hammer, you can try this alternative technique. Set the bevelled edge of a stone hammer at an angle of about 30 degrees, near the bottom of the unwanted section, and chip away small pieces of stone by striking the stone hammer with a club hammer (see illustration left). Work along the lower edge first, chipping off small pieces, then turn the stone and repeat.

Left: *The mortar used for this slate crazy-paving path was coloured to harmonise with the stone. The rectangular area towards the centre waiting to be mortared hides a drain inspection cover and has been laid over a sheet of butyl rubber so that it can easily be lifted if necessary.*

 ### Shaping stone

Always take your time when cutting or shaping stone. Hurried, heavy blows usually mean a collection of assorted rock chips rather than a neatly trimmed shaped piece.

Rectangular paving

Although crazy-paving is appropriate for some situations, rectangular paving slabs may be a more appropriate material for a patio and many other uses.

Many kinds of stone can be cut into relatively thin sections suitable for paving, and your stone merchant or quarry should be able to advise on what's available in your area.

You should be able to buy pieces already cut to rectangles in a variety of sizes. Don't expect them to be perfect, however — slight irregularities in both size and surface are part of the charm of real stone. If you can't find pieces of a particular size or shape, then if necessary you'll have to cut some of them to shape yourself, using an angle grinder (disc cutter).

You should start by preparing a firm base. As stone paving is usually used for decorative paths and patios rather than for drives, the base needs to be firm but not especially substantial.

Excavate the area to be paved, and use edge restraints such as concrete path edging or just strips of wood. Ram about 3 in (8 cm) of hardcore rubble into the base, making sure it's well compacted. Then tip about 5 cm (2 in) of sand over the top, raking and tamping it level so there is a firm sand base.

Crevice plants

The irregular size and shape of natural stone paving slabs means there are sometimes relatively large gaps between the stones. You can fill these with mortar, breaking up a spare slab to produce infill pieces if necessary, but why not use these gaps to provide a footing for plants? You'll need to use suitable plants, and it's sensible only to do this for areas that don't get trodden on much.

Plants that do well in paving include:

- *Campanula cochleariifolia*
- *Campanula portenschlagiana*
- *Erinus alpinus*
- *Mentha requienii*
- *Pratia pedunculata*
- *Sedum* (various species and varieties)
- *Thymus serpyllum* (creeping thyme).

You should find these in the alpine section of a good garden centre.

You can use more vigorous plants such as:

- *Aubrieta* (rock cress)
- *Alyssum saxatile* (now more correctly *Aurinia saxatilis*).

But these need plenty of space and are best trimmed back after flowering.

You can even use some annuals for quick results. Try a compact variety of:

- *Alyssum maritimum* (more correctly *Lobularia maritima*; sweet alyssum)
- *Iberis umbellata* (candytuft)
- *Ionopsidium acaule* (violet cress)
- *Leptosiphon* hybrids (star dust)
- *Limnanthes douglasii* (poached-egg plant).

If the slabs vary in size, lay a few large ones along the edge to start with, making the most of any existing straight edges.

steps continue overleaf

It may be necessary to cut some of the slabs to straighten the edge or simply to get them to fit. You can use an angle grinder (disc cutter), but if you have just a few slabs to cut or trim, there's a simpler method you could use (see illustration).

Score a line using a club hammer and bolster chisel, then gradually deepen the groove until the stone can be split along the line with a sharp blow.

When laying the slabs, it may at times be necessary to add or remove sand to provide a stable, level finish. Mortar is often not needed with large stone slabs, although a few blobs of mortar can sometimes be useful.

Finishing off

Dribble sand in between the stones and press it in firmly with something like a pencil or narrow strip of wood. If you hate the idea of weeds or moss growing in the joints, use mortar instead of sand.

Usually natural gaps are far more acceptable with stone paving than with manufactured slabs, and in areas that won't be trampled you could even sow or plant small but tough alpines in the cracks.

Right: *The irregular size of the slabs, and the random, informal appearance, is part of the charm and appeal of a real stone path.*

Planning a raised bed

A rock or stone raised bed somehow looks more satisfying than one made from bricks, and if you use local stone it will almost certainly blend in with the background and make a well-integrated garden feature.

To get the best from rocks, it's important to let the material dictate the method of construction, so be prepared to modify your plan and some of the construction techniques to suit the type and size of rocks or stones you have available. Flints were used for the round raised bed below, as these are widely available in the part of Sussex where this bed was built. Elsewhere a different stone may be more appropriate.

The size of your raised bed should be in proportion to the size of your garden. Don't make it too large, otherwise it will be expensive to construct and may look out of place. If you want to make a raised bed for alpines, a height of about 18–24 in (45–60 cm) will be sufficient, but for taller plants 36 in (90 cm) may not look out of place in a large garden.

When you're building with stone, a circular bed is often more pleasing than a rectangular one, but in a formal part of the garden straight lines may be more appropriate. The method of construction is similar, though you will obviously have to adapt the instructions accordingly.

Mortared flints

Prepare a firm footing for the wall. If you're building a circular wall, mark out the area to be excavated by inserting a peg in the ground where you want the centre of the circle to be. Loop a piece of string around it, and hold a stick or bottle filled with dry sand within the other end of the loop.

Keeping the string taut, mark out the outer and inner extent of the footing by scribing with the stick or trickling dry sand out of the bottle.

Excavate a trench about 18 in (45 cm) wide and 6 in (15 cm) deep. Insert pegs about 3 ft (1 m) apart all around the trench, then use a spirit-level between them to make sure the tops are at the same height. This is the level to which you will pour the concrete.

A flint wall — or any wall that uses small stones — needs a lot of mortar for support. Unless the wall is wide, this would make it unstable, so you should build an inner wall of bricks or inexpensive low-density walling blocks. For a curved bed it may be necessary to cut the bricks or blocks in half to make it easier to follow the curved footing.

Build about 9–12 in (23–30 cm) of the inner wall, then bank mortar against this into which you can bed the flints or small stones. If you're using flints, try to ensure a broken face is left exposed. Continue with another 9–12 in (23–30 cm) and repeat the process until you reach the required height.

To finish off, extend the mortar over the top and bed capping stones into it.

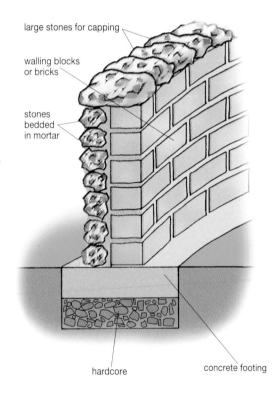

large stones for capping

walling blocks
or bricks

stones
bedded
in mortar

hardcore

concrete footing

Left: *This attractive circular raised bed is faced with flint bedded into mortar. A few planting holes have been left in the side to allow plants such as* Alyssum saxatile *(now more correctly* Aurinia saxatilis*) to be grown.*

Using slabs

Paving stones are another pleasing choice for a raised bed, especially if they blend in with stone paving used for the surrounding area. The raised bed illustrated here is relatively tall, and one only half this height would still look pleasing in a small garden.

It's best to use mortar to secure the slabs, but for a low bed it may be possible to 'dry lay' them, using small fragments wedged in to make the slabs stable, and perhaps with soil used to bind them together. This kind of bonding will ensure there are plenty of planting places!

A firm footing

Mark out the ground and prepare a footing as described on page 25, and allow the concrete to set before laying the stonework.

Use large pieces at the bottom to ensure a stable base, but be sure to put some aside for later courses. You'll also need to put some large slabs aside for the coping.

Use either sifted soil or a mortar mix to bed the pieces firmly. If you are using soil, be prepared to ram in fragments of rock between the larger pieces to make them firm and stable.

Even if the wall itself is not mortared, try to use mortar to fix the coping. The large, flat stones that are placed on top of the wall to cap it are likely to be leaned on or otherwise put under pressure, and if not mortared into position they may become dislodged.

Economical filling

Don't fill your raised bed with poor-quality soil, and be especially careful not to use sub-soil from below the top 12 in (30 cm). Give your plants a chance by using good topsoil or even potting compost for the top 12–18 in (30–45 cm) of your raised bed.

If your bed is deeper than this, place rubble at the bottom (it's a good place to get rid of it, and it will improve drainage), and cover this with any poor soil that you want to get rid of. Compact it well, then top with the better-quality soil or potting compost ready for planting.

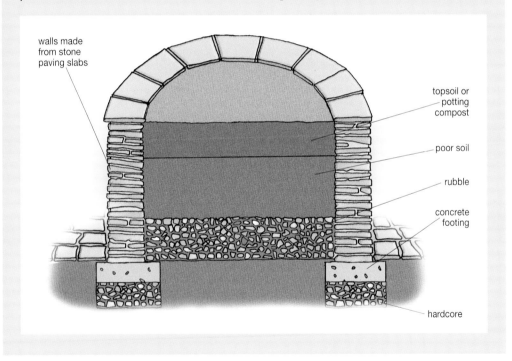

walls made from stone paving slabs

topsoil or potting compost

poor soil

rubble

concrete footing

hardcore

Left: *Stone paving pieces will make a pleasing raised bed, especially if the surrounding path is made from similar stone. Use larger pieces on top to make an attractive and harmonising coping. In a small garden you would have to build on a much smaller scale than here, but the result should be equally effective.*

Cutting and shaping stone

Working with natural stone is a very rewarding activity — but a very challenging one too. Unlike with manufactured products, each piece is slightly different, and it's unlikely that all the pieces will fit without at least some trimming and shaping. This can seem a daunting task, but it's quite easy if you've learned some of the tricks of the trade.

Working with rock is not without hazards, so always take sensible precautions. Don't attempt to lift pieces that are too large to handle on your own (see page 71 for how to handle large rocks safely), and *always* wear goggles and gloves when cutting or shaping rock. Splinters and fragments of rock may fly out even when the cut is a clean one.

Splitting a rock or large stone

Some rocks will split easily along a clearly defined line in the rock, simply by using a stone hammer and sledge hammer as shown in the illustration, applying the pressure in succession in the centre and at both ends. Some rocks are more difficult, and these may require a starter groove made with a bolster chisel or cold chisel and club hammer.

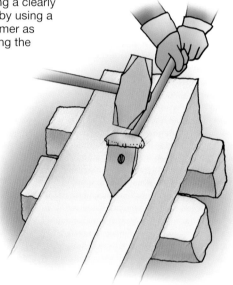

Always try to split a rock along a natural cleavage line. It's easier to find strata lines in some types of rock than in others, but it's usually possible to identify a natural weak point along which you can split the rock.

Support the rock with stones to make it stable, so that it won't roll over or fall when you hit it. Then draw a chalk line where you want to split the rock if the line isn't clearly visible.

Have someone hold the pointed edge of a stone hammer with the bevelled end over the line, near the centre of the rock, then smack the head with a sledge hammer (see illustration). Repeat at both ends and in the centre until a crack begins to open up.

Use a metal wedge, perhaps the head of an old axe, in the centre of the rock, and hit this with a sledge hammer.

Once a crack has been opened up sufficiently, use a crowbar to help lever the split open. Use a to-and-fro movement of the crowbar to lever it apart. Eventually it should split.

Splitting a small stone

Splitting a smaller stone follows the same principles as a larger one, applying pressure from hammer-blows along a natural cleavage, but you can use a bevel-edged stone hammer and a club hammer instead of a sledge hammer.

Removing a corner

Either lay the stone on a bed of sand, or else support it on another rock with the section to be removed overhanging the edge.

Firmly tap the corner to be removed with a stone hammer — but don't give it a great whack, as this will probably cause it to fragment. Chip off small pieces, moving the rock forward occasionally if necessary.

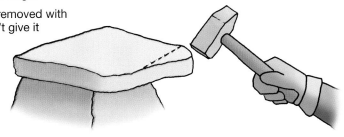

 ## Removing bumps

If there's an inconvenient bump on one face that prevents the rock from bedding snugly into your wall, it may be best to flatten the surface if possible. As bumps are a particular problem if you're laying paving, the method for removing them is described on page 19.

Boundary walls

A stone wall can make your boundary a feature to be admired both from within the garden and from the road. It will be a very public display of your skills, however, so take your time. You can always build a small internal wall within the garden if you feel that you need to practise.

Think carefully about the type of wall you want to build. The picture here shows quite an elaborate stone wall — the use of two different stone types and a curved top adds considerable character but makes it more difficult to construct. If this is your first stone wall, it's a good idea to keep it low, with a level top, and to keep to just one type of stone.

Don't assume, because you're using mortar to bind the stones together, that you don't have to choose the sizes and shapes carefully. It should be the stones and not the mortar that give the wall its strength and stability.

Your wall should be built on a firm foundation. Excavate a trench a little wider than your wall and about 12 in (30 cm) deep.

For a substantial wall, lay a bed of concrete, about 2–3 in (5–8 cm) thick, over a couple of inches of compacted hardcore (rubble). Once this has cured and is hard, bed the first layer of stone on approximately 1 in (2.5 cm) of mortar. (For a low wall just use a bed of mortar.)

Make sure you use large stones for each end — if possible spanning the width of the wall (see illustration). Pack the spaces between the stones with more mortar.

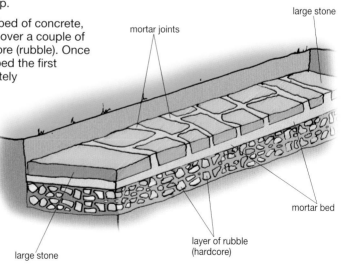

large stone

mortar joints

mortar bed

layer of rubble (hardcore)

large stone

30

This quite elaborate wall has been built from dressed stone, giving it a fairly regular appearance. But a wall this high would be rather too ambitious a project for a beginner — start with something lower and more manageable.

Use a spirit-level against a straight-edge frequently to ensure that the wall is either vertical or tapering inwards slightly towards the top.

Build up the wall a layer at a time, laying about 1 in (2.5 cm) of mortar, then placing the stones. This will compress the mortar so that the final joints may be only half this thickness.

Keep some large flat stones aside to cap the wall. You may be able to obtain large flat stones derived from the same type of rock from your stone merchant.

So that you don't use all the large stones first, and to help create a stronger bond, aim to lay one large stone followed by two smaller ones. On the next row, stagger the sequence so that the two smaller pieces lie over a large one below. You won't be able to follow this unfailingly, but always keep the principle in mind.

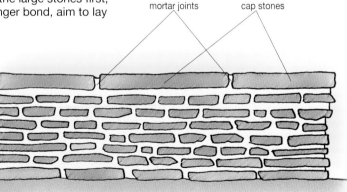

mortar joints   cap stones

Walls to plant in

If you think stone walls sound a bit plain and drab, plant them up with plenty of flowers and foliage. Dry stone walls (see pages 34–37) can be home to lots of plants that thrive if planted in the crevices, but if you want a bigger and bolder show of flowers, it's best to build a wall with a planting cavity.

The illustration below shows a cross-section of a typical stone wall with a planting cavity, though the height, proportions and width of the planting space depend on both the material available and what looks right for the size of your garden.

You can mortar the stones together or lay them dry (in which case you can plant in the sides of the walls too).

If you're using mortar, follow the general advice on pages 30–31; if laying dry, read the advice on pages 34–37. Dry-laid walls should be tapered inwards towards the top, which provides extra stability. Mortared walls, especially if they are low ones, can be built with vertical sides. If you taper the sides, use a home-made batter gauge (see page 36).

To mortar or not to mortar?

The advantage of an unmortared wall is that you can plant the sides with anything from choice alpines to bold and brash spring bloomers such as the yellow gold dust (*Alyssum saxatile*; re-named *Aurinia saxatilis*) and *Aubrieta* with its curtains of flowers in shades of blue and purple.

You can still plant in a mortared wall provided you leave a few planting crevices unmortared, but you need to think about the position of the plants as you build the wall, and it's not so easy to change your mind or add extra planting positions later.

Mortared walls can be made with vertical sides, whereas dry walls need to slope inwards for stability. This means a dry stone wall will be wider at the base than a normal mortared wall, which may be a consideration where space is a problem. Of course, you can taper a mortared wall if you prefer.

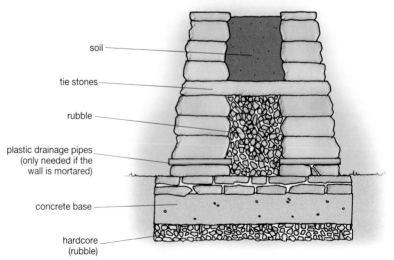

soil

tie stones

rubble

plastic drainage pipes
(only needed if the
wall is mortared)

concrete base

hardcore
(rubble)

You may feel more confident with the knowledge that the stones are firmly bonded with mortar and don't depend just on the laws of gravity for stability.

Weep holes

If you do decide to mortar all the joints, insert a few plastic tubes to act as weep holes to allow surplus water to drain away. Ordinary plastic plumbing pipes are adequate for this purpose, and you only need to insert them every couple of yards (metres).

The pipe does not need to extend beyond the wall. If the end stops just short of the outside, with the stone overhanging it slightly, the pipe won't look obtrusive.

You don't need to make your wall high for it to be effective. This wall, for which dressed stone has been used, with mortared joints, is planted with Juniperus communis *'Compressa',* Thuja orientalis *'Aurea Nana' and* Chamaecyparis lawsoniana *'Minima Glauca'.*

Filling the cavity

Although you can fill the whole cavity with soil, it makes sense to use rubble in the bottom half and soil for the top. This is especially important if you are likely to have to use poor or infertile soil, such as sub-soil. Anything from below the top 9 in (23 cm) of soil is unlikely to support good plant growth unless heavily improved with humus-forming material such as rotted manure or garden compost, and plenty of fertiliser.

As some tie-stones (those that span from one side of the wall to the other) are advisable anyway, you could place them along the length of the wall to support the soil. Inevitably soil will fall down between the stones to fill the space between the rubble, but the wall will still require less soil. Make sure it is tamped well down before planting, otherwise there may be a lot of settlement afterwards.

Dry stone walls

Dry stone walling is an ancient craft that can take years of practice to do rapidly and proficiently. A professional dry stone waller will build a wall with amazing speed, hardly pausing to decide on which stone to use next. For the rest of us there's more trial and error involved, and if you're doing it for pleasure it doesn't matter if it takes a little longer to select and position the best stones. Provided you take your time and aren't over-ambitious, you should be able to produce an attractive and stable wall.

Although we show you the principles here, no two stones are the same, so don't worry if you find it difficult to find stones that look similar to those illustrated. Different kinds of stone have different appearances: sandstones may be large and chunky; slates usually come in flatter sections. Be prepared to work with whatever local stone is available economically.

Remember that building a dry stone wall is not a job for a weekend. Think of it as a project to spread over weeks or even months. If you don't rush it, you'll make a better job of it and probably find it far more satisfying.

How high?

Unless you need a wall to keep animals in or out, then don't try to build it high. A wall 3 ft (90 cm) tall is more than adequate for most purposes, and if you just want an attractive boundary marker, then 2 ft (60 cm) may be enough. Extra height means more cost, effort and time.

For stability, the height of your wall should be about the same as the width at the base (see illustration below).

Building your wall

Even though a dry stone wall may lack the absolutely straight lines and vertical faces of a brick wall, it should still be laid to a straight line, and ideally on a well-prepared footing.

Mark out the area to be excavated for the footing using a garden line and pegs, then excavate a trench about 8 in (20 cm) deep, though a little more or less won't matter. But ensure the bottom of the trench is as flat and level as possible, as you will be laying the foundation stones on this.

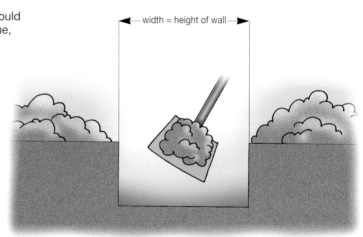

width = height of wall

Choose large, flat stones for each end of the trench, and infill with more large ones to form a firm base for the rest of the wall. Don't forget to put aside enough large, flat stones to cap the wall, however, and you will also need some large ones to use as tie stones.

Your foundation stones should not actually touch. Space them about 1 in (2.5 cm) apart, though of course this may vary. Fill the spaces between with gravel, which will aid drainage as well as providing a firm base.

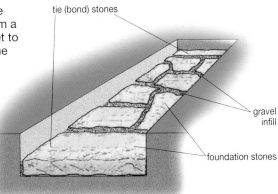

tie (bond) stones

gravel infill

foundation stones

Lay the subsequent stones carefully, choosing a suitable size for each one, and trimming them if necessary. Wherever possible, place two smaller stones over a large one, and a large stone over two small ones.

Each time you've laid a couple of courses, then every yard (metre) or so along the length of the wall, lay a large stone across the full width of the wall. Such stones are called tie stones, or bond stones, because they help to tie or bond the wall together.

tie stones

angle stones towards centre of wall

rubble infill

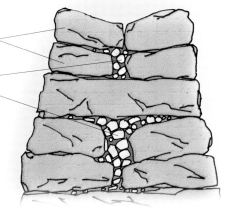

Try to slope the stones towards the centre so that they form a shallow V. You can use small fragments of stone to adjust the angle or to make an uneven stone more stable. Inevitably there will be cracks and crevices, and these should be filled with rubble or small stones.

steps continue overleaf

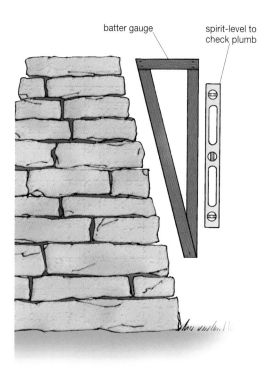

batter gauge

spirit-level to check plumb

Right: *The appearance of a dry stone wall is affected by the type of stone used; whenever possible, try to use stone that occurs naturally in your part of the country. This wall was built in Wales using local slate. Instead of the usual flat coping, the pieces have been stood on end for a more decorative effect. But this is a less stable form of coping than the more traditional horizontal form.*

Batter gauge

Your wall should also slope inwards towards the top, and the best way to ensure that you maintain a fairly even angle is to make a batter gauge (see illustration left).

Simply nail three battens of scrap wood together to give a slope of about 1 in 12 (5°). When you use the gauge, place a spirit-level against it to check it's vertical.

cap stone

Cap stones

Use large, flat stones for the capping at the top. If these are heavy,don't attempt to lift them by yourself. Get help, and if necessary use rollers on a board (see illustration opposite).

Raising heavy stones

Don't struggle trying to lift heavy stones to a height. Use a strong plank on a stable support, and use a crowbar to move the stone on rollers (lengths of steel pipe are suitable). It's still hazardous to do this on your own, in case you lose control, so always have a helper.

crowbar

steel pipes or rollers

stout plank

wooden log

A retaining bank

Retaining banks are sometimes a necessity if your garden is on a sloping site, either to produce terraces or to hold back the soil where you want a path or paved area.

Retaining walls for very steep banks — and especially where a wall more than about 4 ft (1.2 m) high is required — are best left for professionals to build. But a small retaining wall, in an area where a collapse would not risk causing injury or damage, should be easy and safe for you to build yourself.

Although a mortared wall will be stronger, a dry stone retaining wall provides many more planting opportunities. Plants can help to make a large retaining wall less oppressive and visually much more interesting. As a compromise, you could use some mortar but leave the exposed face unmortared, with plenty of planting spaces.

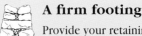

A firm footing

Provide your retaining wall with a firm footing, ideally a concrete base over compacted hardcore. You might get away with rubble or compacted hardcore alone if the wall is relatively low, in which case use large flat stones for the base.

Make sure the base of the wall starts below ground level.

Before you start to build the wall, you should first work out how far back you're going to have to cut into the bank, and where you're going to put the soil you'll need to remove. If you're building a series of terraces you may be able to use the surplus soil to top up a lower level, but if you're planning to grow plants rather than pave the area, be sure to keep the topsoil on the surface. The much less fertile sub-soil will

create major problems for most plants. If some sub-soil does end up near the surface, then adding lots of organic material such as rotted manure and garden compost will help to improve the structure and raise fertility.

Cut further into the bank than the intended width of the wall, as you will need to backfill with some material such as gravel or rubble to ensure good drainage. Slope the sides into the bank in order to reduce the risk of the wall collapsing during construction while it is still unsupported.

Before laying the wall, you should first make a batter gauge (see page 36) with a backwards slope of approximately 1 in for every 1 ft height (2.5 cm for every 30 cm). Use this frequently as the wall is erected, to make sure it has an adequate slope into the bank.

You can lay the stone dry, rather like one-half of a dry stone wall (see pages 34–37), but it's advisable to mortar the stones into position for additional strength. You can always leave areas unmortared on the face, where you can pack in enough soil for suitable plants to take hold.

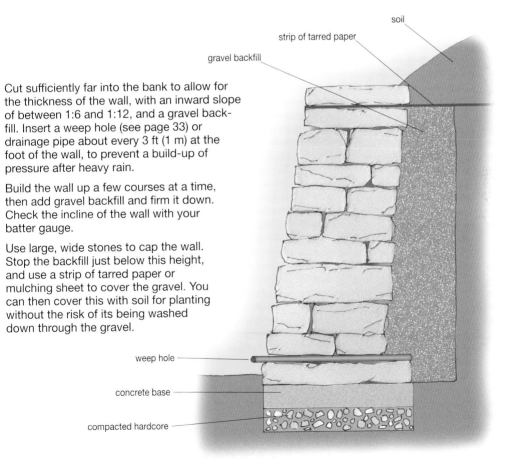

soil

strip of tarred paper

gravel backfill

Cut sufficiently far into the bank to allow for the thickness of the wall, with an inward slope of between 1:6 and 1:12, and a gravel backfill. Insert a weep hole (see page 33) or drainage pipe about every 3 ft (1 m) at the foot of the wall, to prevent a build-up of pressure after heavy rain.

Build the wall up a few courses at a time, then add gravel backfill and firm it down. Check the incline of the wall with your batter gauge.

Use large, wide stones to cap the wall. Stop the backfill just below this height, and use a strip of tarred paper or mulching sheet to cover the gravel. You can then cover this with soil for planting without the risk of its being washed down through the gravel.

weep hole

concrete base

compacted hardcore

A low retaining wall for a bed

Gently sloping ground provides a wonderful opportunity to build low retaining walls that function like low raised beds on level ground, adding lots of visual interest in the process.

A low retaining wall of about 1–2 ft (30–60 cm) is often sufficient to level a gentle slope, and it's a simple walling project that nevertheless looks impressive.

These low retaining walls can be mortared, but it's often unnecessary, and if the stones are reasonably flat and stack easily you may find a dry-laid wall visually more appealing. Certainly it will give you an opportunity to plant in the face if you want to pack in plenty of plants. But even mortared low retaining walls without plants can be pleasing to look at, as they are unlikely to look oppressive in the way that a high wall can sometimes appear.

Low retaining walls can safely be laid dry and planted up with small rock plants to soften the effect, but consider mortaring stones that are very uneven in size. Some types of low stone wall look best capped with larger stones, others can be left uncapped.

Building the wall

First clear the site and cut back into the bank far enough to give you a reasonable working space. Unlike the higher wall described on pages 38–39, a low one like this should not require any backfilling with drainage material such as gravel.

Produce a firm, level base for your wall. If the ground is soft or unstable, ram hardcore rubble into it to provide a stable base. If the ground is firm and compacted, just make sure it's level.

Laying will be easier if you choose reasonably flat stones of an even thickness, but more random stones can be used if you ram rubble between them to provide stability.

If you plan to plant up the wall, use a thin sprinkling of sifted soil between the stones to help bed them in firmly. You can even insert small plants as you progress, which you may find easier than trying to plant later.

Check periodically to ensure that your wall is level, especially when you reach the final course, using a spirit-level on a long straight-edged piece of wood.

Making steps

Stone steps have a timeless appeal and blend in harmoniously with most garden settings. They can become a focal point in their own right, as well as serving a practical purpose.

Making stone steps is likely to prove more difficult than using paving slabs for the treads and bricks or walling blocks for the risers — but the results are usually well worth the extra care needed in selecting and fitting stones of a suitable size.

Piecing together random stones to produce a flight of stable and attractive steps is a little like doing a jigsaw puzzle, but you can make the job easier by using stone that is cut into relatively thin layers and sold primarily for paving. Slates and sandstones are sometimes available that are suitably thin and easy to work with.

For some tips on the best dimensions for your steps, turn to page 44.

Decorative steps

Most steps are built to link terraces or different parts of the garden on a sloping site. But if your garden is fairly flat and you still fancy a flight of steps, just be a little inventive.

By creating a mound of soil backed by shrubs it's easy to create the illusion of a sloping site that justifies your steps. But you'll need to include a small paved area at the top, perhaps with a seat, to provide a sense of purpose.

Steps like this are best made broad, perhaps with a sweeping curved front, and the treads can be shallow if you want to create the illusion of a tall flight even though the height scaled is modest.

Making your steps wide means you can more easily grow lots of paving plants in the crevices without making them look cluttered or hazardous. It may even be possible to include small ornaments on one side for added interest.

How to make stone steps

Mark the approximate position of each step with string stretched between pegs, making sure the vertical height between each string is constant. You can make some adjustment by making the treads deeper (see the panel on page 44 for a guide to the ideal dimensions). When you're happy with the spacing, cut out the shape of the steps roughly using a spade.

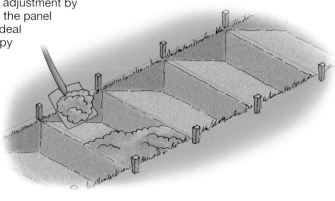

It's advisable to bed the first step on a concrete footing, so you should remove about 6–8 in (15–20 cm) of soil where the bottom riser will be, and fill the hole with about 4 in (10 cm) of concrete over a layer of compacted hardcore.

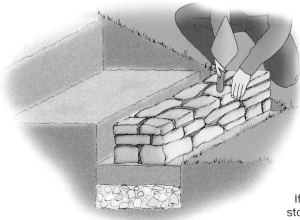

Lay the first riser, choosing stones that are similar in thickness if possible. Make sure a flat face points outwards (it won't matter if the inner face is uneven as this won't be seen).

If you're using fairly flat paving stones, it may be possible to lay them dry without mortaring. But if the stones are uneven in thickness, or have a very uneven top or bottom surface, it's best to mortar them into position. This will make it much easier to ensure that the risers are level enough to support a stable tread. Use a spirit-level to check that the step is level.

Terms explained

The **riser height** is the vertical distance from one step to the next. About 6 in (15 cm) makes the climb comfortable, but if the slope is steep you may have to increase this.

The **tread depth** is the horizontal distance from the front of the step (including any overhang) to the next riser.

step-by-step description continues overleaf

43

Right: *Stone steps are usually more ornamental than those made from concrete blocks or bricks, and often become a focal point in their own right.*

Backfill any space behind the riser with gravel, and ram it down to consolidate it. Choose large, flat pieces of stone for the treads. It may be necessary to cut very irregular pieces into an appropriate rectangle. For stability and safety, it's a good idea to bed the stones on a few blobs of mortar.

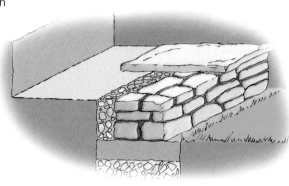

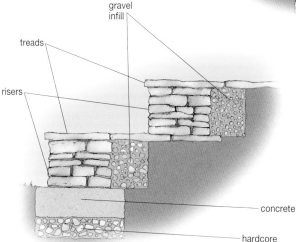

gravel
infill

treads

risers

Build the next riser towards the back of the tread of the first step, and proceed to build the whole flight in the same way. Overlap the tread by about 1 in (2.5 cm), and make sure the depth of the tread from the front to the next riser is constant for each step.

concrete

hardcore

Ideal dimensions

So that your steps look in proportion and are easy to use, you should try to keep within the guidelines that have been shown by experience to work well.

A riser height of about 6 in (15 cm) and a tread depth of about 15 in (38 cm) make a good starting point, although you may have to modify this slightly.

For comfort, try to make the riser at least 4 in (10 cm) and not more than 7 in (16.5 cm) high. For similar reasons, the treads should not be less than 11 in (28 cm) deep.

Steps with a difference

Stone steps are always unique: each type of rock used has its own individual characteristics, and no two pieces of stone are exactly the same, so your steps will be made from a jigsaw of different pieces. And there are other ways of making your steps distinctive, too.

Quick and easy steps

If you have a grassy slope, perhaps in a wild garden or in a woodland garden, stone steps cut into the bank can make a pleasing feature. It's a quick and easy project and won't require a lot of stone.

If the grass is long, cut it before you start the project to make the work easier. Then work out the position of the base of each step, inserting small wooden pegs as markers at each side. The height and angle of the slope will determine the exact spacing, but for comfort, try to make the risers at least 4 in (10 cm) high but not more than 8 in (20 cm). For steps that will not be used frequently, a steeper 10 in (25 cm) spacing may be acceptable, though they will be hard to climb.

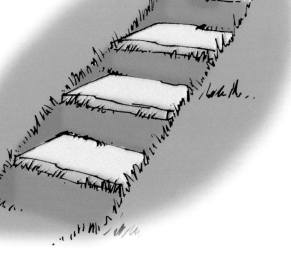

Choose large, flat stones for comfort and appearance.

Starting at the bottom, cut into the bank with a spade, using your intended stone as a guide for the depth and width. Achieving a firm fit is a matter of trial and error, removing or adding soil as necessary. A supply of sand is useful for levelling the base.

Don't leave an overhang at the edge, as you would for normal steps: not being mortared or fixed to a firm base, the stone could tip.

Slice the ground vertically above your step, using the spade, to produce a definite step rather than a sloping riser. Grass will soon regrow, but if erosion is likely, simply use turf sliced off the next step to pack against the riser. Keep it watered in dry weather until the roots grow into the bank.

Finishing touches

Stone steps lend themselves to a little floral or foliage decoration, especially if they're wide. The gaps between the treads, or between tread and riser, are sometimes relatively wide, thereby providing a plentiful foothold for many kinds of small rock plants.

Many of these, such as *Campanula* and *Aubrieta* (see picture above), are best started off from seed: just pack some good soil into the appropriate crevices and sow a tiny pinch of seed. Keep them watered — preferably by spraying with a mister rather than using a watering can or hose, to reduce the risk of washing the seeds away — then you'll soon have seedlings that will look after themselves.

Confine your plants to the crevices at the back of the treads, so that they grow up in front of the risers, or at the sides. It's inadvisable to allow plants (whether desirable or weeds) to grow between crevices that you might step on, as there's the risk of someone slipping on them.

The risers on these steps have been planted with Aubrieta, *which would make a wonderful display even with less elaborate steps.*

Woody plants

Shrubs or woody climbers sound unlikely plants to grow on steps, yet if planted at the bottom or side, some can be trained to run along the risers. Ivies (*Hedera*) are sometimes used in this way, but even the Virginia creeper (*Parthenocissus quinquefolia*) and Boston ivy (*P. tricuspidata*) can be used, though these are more appropriate if the steps flank a wall covered with the same creeper.

A more restrained choice is *Cotoneaster horizontalis*, which with patience and care can be trained along the risers. The small deep-green leaves look pleasing all summer, and in autumn the bright red berries can be stunning.

All these plants must be trimmed regularly to keep them looking neat, and to prevent stems or leaves making the paths hazardous to use.

Formal gravel gardens

If you're fed up with mowing the lawn, then why not replace the grass with gravel? It will look good, and you won't have to use the lawn-mower any more!

A gravel garden like the one pictured below is a relatively quick and easy project if you just want to replace an existing lawn with gravel. Because a mulching sheet or black plastic sheet is used beneath the gravel, you shouldn't even have to worry about weeds.

Gravel isn't as boring as it might sound. You may miss the lush green of a lawn in spring and early summer, but during those hot summer months it will look far better than a drought-scorched lawn. You'll also begin to appreciate the many subtle shades of gravel — the colours

appear to change according to the intensity of the light and whether the gravel is wet or dry.

You can plant through gravel to add a touch of colour — this technique is described on pages 52-53. However, if you're just replacing grass with gravel and want to retain the existing shape and structure, especially if there are flower beds in the lawn, it's best to leave the gravel simply as a texture and confine the plantings to the flower beds.

Left: *This gravelled area was previously a lawn, but the owner wanted something that demanded less maintenance. The garden has even been trans-formed without disturbing the established flower beds, which remain in exactly the same position as they did beforehand.*

Creating a gravel garden

Bed a concrete edging strip (you could use concrete coping stones) around the edge to contain the gravel. If a wide border bounds the area, you may be able to take a little space from the border and bed the edging on compacted rubble or gravel. Check the levels, and fix the edging with a few blobs of mortar for extra stability and strength. Alternatively, remove a little soil from around the edge of the old lawn and fix the edging in the same way.

Killing the grass

Digging up an established lawn can be hard, tedious work. You may prefer to take a short-cut.

First kill the grass with a weedkiller (not a selective hormone lawn weedkiller, of course!). If you're not planning to plant through the gravel it doesn't matter if you use a persistent type, but if there's any likelihood of planting use a non-persis-tent systemic weedkiller.

When the grass is dead you can begin laying the gravel. To save time and effort, you can simply use edging stones around the old grassed area and lay your gravel in the area bounded by the edging. Alternatively, slice off the top 2 in (5 cm) or so of the old lawn with a spade, and lower the edging accordingly.

Don't bother to dig over the area as it will be covered anyway, and firm compacted ground forms a better base than freshly dug soil.

steps continue overleaf

49

Slice off about 2 in (5 cm) from the old lawn once the grass has been killed, and roughly level the ground. You don't have to make it exactly level, because any slight irregularities will be masked by the gravel.

Lay a mulching sheet or thick black polythene sheet over the consolidated ground. This is unlikely to be wide enough to cover the whole area, so simply overlap the strips by about 2 in (5 cm). Although not an essential measure, using a sheet like this will reduce the risk of weeds growing through the gravel later on.

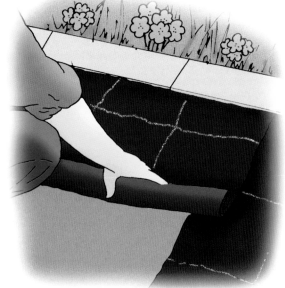

Obtaining gravel

Small pea-sized gravel or shingle is widely available from builders' merchants. On the other hand, you'll find a much wider range sold by large garden centres and specialist stone companies. But beware: buying a large quantity of gravel in small bags can work out expensive. If you need a lot of gravel, try to negotiate a special price or ask for quotations from companies who deliver in bulk.

The drawback of a lorry delivery of loose gravel is moving it. If they tip it on the road, you'll need to make arrangements to move it quickly so that it doesn't cause an obstruction. Have it tipped on your drive if possible.

Choosing gravel

Gravel varies considerably in size and shape. Some gravels are fairly rounded, while others are rough and angular. The colour of gravel depends on the rock from which it has been derived: some gravels are pale (sometimes glaringly so), while others are more mellow — and you can even find 'green' and 'red' gravels.

Large garden centres often have a display of samples, which makes it easier to choose the right one. But it's worth buying a bag and spreading the gravel over a small area first — just to see what it looks like in your garden, in different lights, and when dry and wet.

Barrow the gravel into position, and rake it level. Make sure it is no higher than the edging, otherwise it may accidentally be kicked onto the flower beds.

Informal gravel gardens

Gravel is ideal for carpeting the ground in an informal garden. It easily flows to fill irregular shapes, and it makes a pleasing backdrop for plants that cascade and tumble over the edge. You can even plant through the gravel to create a natural-looking effect whereby plants and gravel become part of an integrated picture.

Even an informal area needs boundaries to enclose the gravel. A sunken area is ideal if bounded by a low wall. Otherwise, perimeter paths can form a natural boundary, with beds created by planting through the gravel. If you do this, leave gravelled areas that form meandering paths between the planted areas.

Excavate the soil to allow for a layer of gravel about 2 in (5 cm) thick. If you're planning to plant though the gravel, make sure the soil is well dug and manured or fertilised, and allow the ground to settle and consolidate it before proceeding.

Cover the ground with a mulching sheet or heavy-duty black polythene sheet (see illustration). If some joins are needed, simply overlap the edges by about 2 in (5 cm).

Barrow the gravel to various points and tip it in heaps initially, raking small areas as you work from one side. Finally, rake the whole area level.

A large area of gravel can be improved by planting through it, preferably in bold groups rather than as numerous isolated plants.

Plants that are good in gravel

- *Armeria maritima*
- *Dianthus* (alpine types)
- *Helianthemum nummularium*
- *Oenothera missouriensis* (syn. *O. macrocarpa*)
- *Persicaria affinis* (syn. *Polygonum affine*)
- *Phlox douglasii*
- *Saxifraga* (mossy types)
- *Silene schafta*
- *Thymus serpyllum*
- *Veronica prostrata*

To plant through the gravel, simply draw back an area large enough for the size of the root-ball, and cut two slits in the polythene in the form of a cross, using a sharp knife or scissors.

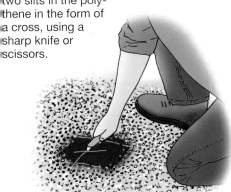

Plant normally, but with the top of the root-ball a little above the soil if the crown would be buried when you return the gravel. Firm in well, pull the gravel back, and water well.

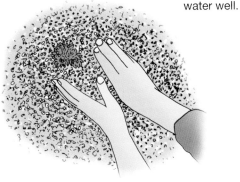

Stone gardens

If you want to make a bolder statement than a gravel garden, you could consider a stone garden. The principle is similar except that this time large stones, pebbles and rocks are used, often in a creative or 'architectural' way.

Although the principles of a stone garden can be explained, the actual design and construction has to be modified to suit the materials available as well as your own design preferences. Let the rocks or stones dictate the form and shape, and arrange them in a way that looks pleasing as well as striking.

Your stone garden should be a strong visual feature and not just a background for plants. Plants are usually required to remove any suggestion of harshness or monotony, but it's best to choose those that have a strong profile or architectural quality, such as bamboos, distinctive grasses, and perhaps succulents.

Line your stone garden with a mulching sheet or heavy-duty black polythene sheet to prevent any weed growth; you can always plant through the sheet by making a cross-slit with a knife or scissors.

Try to use a variety of stone sizes to add interest, and don't be afraid to use more than one kind of stone. Large beach pebbles — obtainable from stone merchants and large garden centres — are a good choice for the basic cover, but you can try adding some large feature rocks or big boulders to provide some extra interest.

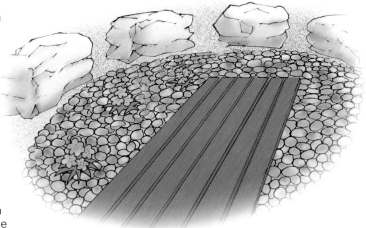

You don't have to confine yourself to stones for the hard landscaping: timber decking often makes a happy marriage with the stone in this kind of garden.

Plants that are super with stones

- *Aeonium arboreum* (not hardy)
- *Agave americana* 'Variegata' (not hardy)
- *Artemisia schmidtiana* 'Nana'
- *Festuca glauca*
- *Foeniculum vulgare*
- *Imperata cylindrica*
- *Ophiopogon planiscapus* 'Nigrescens'
- *Phormium* (dwarf hybrids)
- *Schizostylis coccinea*
- *Sedum* (alpine and herbaceous species)
- *Sempervivum*
- *Stipa gigantea*

Left: *Timber decking can look really stunning as part of a stone garden, because it adds another different texture and usually brings a little more colour.*

Below: *Succulent plants such as agaves look just right in a dry, rocky setting. If they're not hardy, grow them in pots that you can take under cover for winter.*

A rock cascade

Rock and water are natural companions, and although you can't construct a real mountain stream in your garden, the essential elements and an illusion of the wild are something that it's easy to create, even in a small garden.

If your garden is on a slope, this is an excellent project, because a watercourse with tumbling cascades should look very natural. You'll also have less earth-moving to do.

A flat site means you have to build an artificial mound, but you can use the soil excavated from the 'stream' to help build up the bank. It doesn't have to be high (a big bank in a small garden may look wrong); just make the drops for the falls shallower. In a small garden a cascade with a 6-in (15-cm) drop can look and sound as pleasing as a 12-in (30-cm) fall in a grander setting.

Decide what your water course will look like *before* you begin excavating. You will need a deep header pool that holds a generous reservoir of water, a bottom pool with a pump to return water to the header pool, and a series of cascades to link them. You'll have to think about laying on the power supply and burying the hose before you start to lay the liner.

Buying a liner

Don't skimp or economise on the liner. You'll be placing heavy and perhaps sharp rocks on it, and there's a risk of a thin or economy liner being punctured. And if you do have a puncture somewhere, lifting heavy rocks to find it will soon convince you that it's wise to go for the best.

Butyl rubber is very long-lasting, is easy to work with because it has more 'stretch' than most other liners, and is unlikely to disappoint. But beware: it comes in various thicknesses, and economy-quality butyl liners may be thinner than desirable for this kind of project. Don't skimp on this part of your investment.

Most pre-cut liners come in sizes ideal for ordinary ponds but inappropriate for a 'stream'. For this you need a long, narrow liner, and that usually means ordering it from a specialist aquatic supplier. Appropriate companies will supply a liner to any size, though you may have to give them a few days' notice.

The method shown below is only suitable where there is a small difference in height between header and bottom pool. For a steeper drop, turn to page 59.

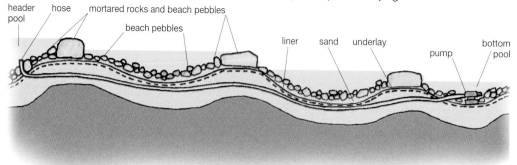

header pool | hose | mortared rocks and beach pebbles
beach pebbles
liner | sand | underlay | pump | bottom pool

Excavate the basic shape of your stream, bearing in mind the tips given in the previous step, and then line the excavation with a pond underlay. You can buy these from aquatic suppliers, and they will help to protect your liner.

Drape the liner over the excavation and mould it into the cavity as best you can. The weight of the water will force it into shape as it's filled. Don't worry about a few creases, these will hardly be noticed once your stream is edged and filled with water.

Check that both sides of the liner are level. This is important, otherwise you'll have water seeping away.

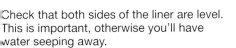

steps continue overleaf

57

Pump power

The best-made stream will be a failure if your pump isn't powerful enough to sustain the required flow of water. You may require a powerful mains-voltage pump. Consult an expert at an aquatic centre, and be prepared to give the dimensions of your widest cascade. If you also need to run a biological filter from your pump, extra power may be required to feed this too.

An ordinary hosepipe of the kind used for watering the garden will probably be inadequate. Large-diameter pipes will be required to move enough water, so look into these aspects before you start construction.

Making dams

You will have to mortar the rocks into position to form a dam, otherwise water will simply flow under and around the rocks. Use a waterproofing additive to the mixture. This may not produce a totally waterproof seal, but the seepage should be minimal.

Trim surplus liner from the edges, but leave on at least 6 in (15 cm) more than you'll think you'll need. Don't do any final trimming until the stream is complete, and even then it's better to hide the surplus than to cut it off.

Mask the sides with rocks. Small rocks and pebbles can simply be laid on the liner, perhaps bedded on sand, but use a spare offcut of liner beneath any large rock as extra protection.

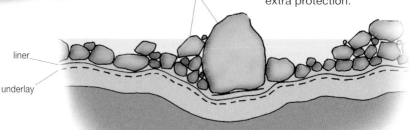

rocks

liner

underlay

Bigger falls

If your stream has cascades with steep drops, or if the vertical distance from head-er to bottom pool is too great to make a stream from a single liner with dams, then you should use the type of con-struction shown here.

Make your stream from a series of separate pools, overlapping the liners as shown so as to ensure that the cascades remain watertight. Slope the channels so that water is retained in each section when the pump is turned off.

Above: *A feature like this makes the most of two natural elements: rock and water. In the process it creates that magical sight and sound of moving water.*

Traditional rock banks

It's surprising that people don't construct more rock gardens than they do. Such gardens make a pleasing focal-point feature, and because alpine plants are usually small you can pack plenty of them into a small space.

If you have a naturally sloping garden, a rock bank can be an excellent way of dealing with a part of the garden that's too steep for a lawn and yet difficult to cultivate as a normal flower bed. You can, of course, build an artificial bank, although for a relatively flat site you may prefer to consider an island bed (see pages 64-65).

It's impossible to give precise instructions for building a rock garden, because every piece of rock is different, just as every site is different too. However, the basic principles described here should be capable of being adapted to suit your particular situation.

 Rocks for a rock garden

Although most kinds of rock can be used very effectively, it's generally better if possible to keep to one that's quarried locally. It will blend in with the local landscape more readily, it's likely to be cheaper because transport costs are less, and you may be able to deal direct with the quarry. This may be especially useful if you want some very large pieces, as you may be able to earmark specific rocks.

Your local garden centre may stock a small range of suitable rocks, though these will tend to be relatively small pieces. A stone merchant is always worth visiting.

Bear in mind that, in a well-constructed rock garden, a large proportion of a particular rock may be hidden below the surface, so that what seems like a large amount of rock may not go as far as you anticipate.

Start building at the bottom of the slope, positioning a row of rocks so that any strata lines flow in the same direction.

To make the rocks look more natural, you may have to dig into the bank to make pockets for them, ensuring that each one slopes backwards and down-wards slightly.

Mix a supply of soil to pack around the rocks as you work. Use a mixture of equal parts of topsoil, coarse grit and peat (or peat substitute).

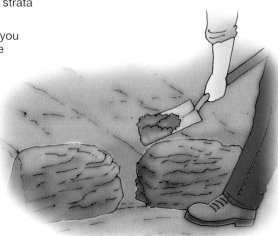

Natural angles

Try to arrange your rocks so they look like natural outcrops. This will involve sloping the rocks at a slight angle as shown below, and being careful to align strata lines in the rock whenever possible (these may not be obvious in some rocks).

Position the next row of rocks, levering them into position. If lifting large rocks, be sure to have someone help you: see page 71 for tips on moving rocks.

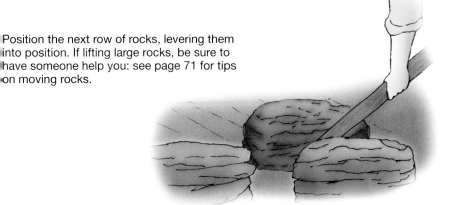

steps continue overleaf

ROCK AND WATER

Safety first

Building a rock garden can be hazardous if you approach the job with a careless attitude. Never try to lift rocks that are too heavy for you, always use your knees to take the strain and not your back, and be sure to enlist help if in any doubt.

For very large rocks you may need mechanical help. Professionals use small cranes or other powered lifting devices for moving large rocks, so consider hiring help if necessary.

For tips on how to move large rocks that are not too large to be manhandled, turn to page 71.

Build the rock garden layer by layer, working up the slope, trying to keep the strata lines aligned, and leaving plenty of planting spaces (see the panel on natural angles on page 61).

Shovel more of the prepared soil mixture around the rocks as you work. Don't worry if a lot of the rock appears to be covered; this will help your rocks look more like natural outcrops.

To avoid large air pockets that could cause the roots to dry out when you plant up your rock bank, consolidate the ground with an old dibber — or perhaps even a piece of scrap wood.

Right: *You may have a broad grassy slope on which to create a rock garden, or barely enough scope for a low bank in a small back yard — but whichever is the case, there's always scope for the imaginative use of rock.*

Planting pockets

Don't forget to leave plenty of planting pockets. Lots of alpine plants grow well in crevices between rocks. Instead of placing one rock directly on top of another, consider inserting a few small fragments of rock and packing the space created with soil.

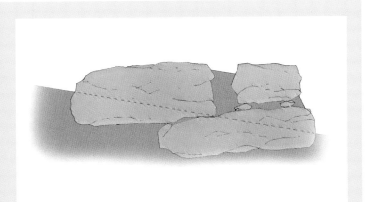

Island rock beds

If you don't have a natural bank on which to build a rock garden, consider making an island rock bed in your lawn. This will help to break up a large and potentially boring expanse of grass, and probably won't demand as much rock as a traditional rock garden.

This simple project can probably be finished in a weekend once you have all the materials together. And you won't need very large rocks for a feature like this, so you shouldn't have to struggle with the weight-lifting. Nevertheless, it's a good idea to have help on hand.

Apart from the rocks, you'll need to have a supply of soil handy as you'll be raising the bed above its original level. You can use ordinary soil, but it's worth mixing a supply of equal parts of topsoil, coarse grit and peat (or peat substitute).

Mark out the shape of the bed with a hosepipe or length of rope. Stand back and view it from different angles — perhaps from an upstairs window if you have one — and adjust the size or shape if necessary. Once you're satisfied, start to dig up the turf inside the marked area.

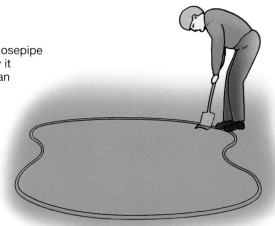

Build the bed in layers, starting around the edge. Try to keep any strata lines in one direction and facing the same way. Angling the rocks down at the back, so that they slope into the soil, will make them look more natural. Use a crowbar or lever to position and adjust heavy rocks.

Finishing touches

Your rock bed will look better, and more natural, if you cover the exposed soil with stone chippings or fine gravel. You can spread this over the soil first, and plant through it, or plant first and then trickle the chippings or gravel between the plants to cover the surface.

If you have a large lawn, an island rock bed will help to break it up visually and provide a useful focal point. Even in a small bed, you should have space for a surprisingly large and interesting collection of alpines.

Don't make a pyramid. A relatively flat top often looks better, and plenty of soil and planting spaces will make an attractive feature once all the plants have grown.

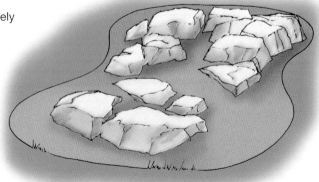

A Mediterranean-style pond

By choosing a warm-coloured rock and adding suitable ornaments and plants, you can build a raised pond that will give your garden a hint of the Mediterranean.

To economise on the amount of rock required for this project, it's sensible to have part of your pond below ground level. That way you'll have a good depth of water without having to build high walls.

This kind of feature pond can easily be adapted to suit the size of your garden, and a small one will look good even in a modest patio.

It's always worth adding a few fish, if only to keep down pests like gnat and mosquito larvae, but this kind of pond relies mostly on coloured stone, reflections, and the sight and sound of moving water for its impact.

How you treat the surrounding area will also influence the type of atmosphere you manage to create. If you want to give it a Mediterranean feel, use plenty of gravel or materials that suggest a dry micro-climate, and plants associated with warm, dry climates, such as herbs, succulents and bedding plants like pelargoniums (bedding geraniums). The lavish use of terracotta containers and ornaments will add to the ambience.

Give your garden some style with a rock-faced raised pond like this. It's sure to attract favourable attention and give your garden that touch of distinction.

Mark out the shape of your pond and excavate to a depth of about 1 ft (30 cm) if you want a pond about 2 ft (60 cm) deep. For a deeper pond, just increase the depth of your excavation.

Always make sure the ground is firm and free from sharp stones or large tree roots.

If you want to grow marginal or aquatic plants around the edge, allow for a edge about 9 in (23 cm) wide. The existing ground level can be used for this purpose.

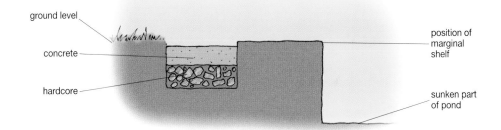

ground level

concrete

hardcore

position of marginal shelf

sunken part of pond

Choosing stone

It's best to visit a stone merchant to see what's available in your area, but as a guide 'cold'-looking rocks such as grey granites are best avoided. Sandstones are usually a good choice, and some of these have a warm, reddish colouring that's especially appealing.

Avoid very large stones, as you'll need lots of small ones for a curved wall like the one illustrated opposite.

Make a footing for the walls, using about 3 in (8 cm) of concrete over a similar depth of compacted hardcore or gravel. Substantial foundations are not required provided that the wall is not high. Smooth the surface level, with the top just below the surrounding ground so that the first course of stones is bedded just below ground level.

steps continue overleaf

Build an inner wall of bricks or blocks to water height. They may have to be cut to make smaller units if the curve is sharp, and must be mortared into position. When calculating how high to build the bricks or blocks, bear in mind that the inner wall will be capped with stone.

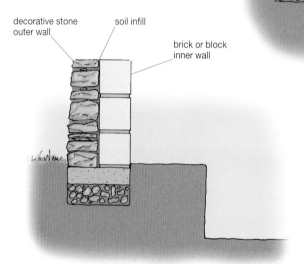

brick or block inner wall

decorative stone outer wall

soil infill

brick or block inner wall

Use the decorative rocks for the outer skin, leaving a small planting cavity between, filling this with soil as you work. This outer wall can be left unmortared so that plants can be grown in the crevices. It also looks more appealing if laid dry. For greater stability, slope the outer wall inwards slightly, and use small broken pieces of rock as wedges if necessary to ensure that the large stones are stable.

Adding movement

Always try to introduce moving water to this kind of pond. It adds to the atmosphere and seems so refreshing on a hot summer's day.

The easiest and cheapest way to introduce the sight and sound of moving water is to buy a small low-voltage submersible pump with a fountain head. Simply plug it in and adjust the fountain head to produce a pattern that you find pleasing.

Water that pours from a figure or ornament can be far more dramatic, however, as you can see from the picture on page 66. You'll almost certainly find the investment adds so much more to your pond.

You can make your own feature out of a pump and some plumbing, with a little drilling and the use of sealants. On the other hand, it's much easier to buy one that comes as a kit.

To protect the liner, use a polyester underlay, which you can buy from aquatic specialists. Just overlap the strips by approximately 2 in (5 cm) where necessary.

Lay the liner, adjusting it as water runs in and moulds it to the contours. Fold neat pleats where appropriate to reduce the number of large creases, though these will hardly be noticed when the pond is finished.

Take the liner over the inner wall, and trim it so that the edge can be mortared beneath the final layer of stone that will be used as a decorative coping.

Finish the wall by using large, flat pieces of the same stone that you used to build the outer wall. Maintain the small planting cavity, but hide the inner brick or block wall with the stone coping.

If you wish, and if it's appropriate for your garden, you can build a higher raised wall of the same stone at the back, as in the photograph on page 66.

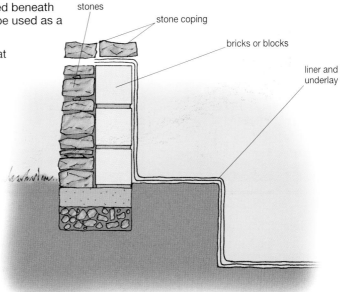

stones

stone coping

bricks or blocks

liner and underlay

Miniature rock gardens

How to improve a glazed sink

There's no excuse for not trying this project. Even if you only have a balcony, you've got space for this kind of rock garden, and with so few rocks to buy it won't cost much either!

You could make a miniature rock garden in a tiny bed in the garden, or use any container that will hold a small amount of soil and that looks sufficiently in harmony with the plants, but stone sinks are the traditional choice.

Genuine stone sinks are expensive and difficult to obtain, but reconstituted stone replicas are sold for just this kind of project. You can also convert an old glazed sink (see panel).

Partly fill the container with a good loam-based potting soil, then arrange your rocks. How you do this depends on the material available and your own artistic flair. Follow the same principles as advised for a full-sized rock garden: make sure the bottoms of the rocks are plunged well into the soil and don't appear to be sitting on top, and try to maintain angles and strata lines running in one direction.

Some enthusiasts like to arrange lots of small rock fragments to create a miniature landscape; others prefer just a few large pieces of rock with plenty of planting crevices.

Clean the glazed area thoroughly, using a detergent to remove any traces of grease, then brush on a PVA adhesive and allow it to become tacky (this takes about 10 minutes). Coat the outside edges, the rim, and the inside to a depth of about 1 in (2.5 cm) from the rim.

While the adhesive is becoming tacky, mix 1 part of coarse sand, 1 part of cement and 2 parts of moistened sieved sphagnum peat together – first dry, and then with some water until it assumes a doughy consistency.

Wearing waterproof gloves, slap this onto the glue-coated surface, pressing on firmly. The layer should be about 0.5 in (12 mm) thick.

Do not fill or plant for at least a week.

Interesting miniature landscapes can be created with rocks and tiny alpine plants. A feature like this will add considerable interest to your patio.

Moving and lifting rocks

Don't be put off building some of the things in this book because you're worried about lifting heavy weights. There are tips and techniques that will make the job much easier.

If you have a medical reason why lifting rocks (even light ones) would not be a good idea, don't even try. Some of the techniques suggested here will make the job easier, but can still cause a strain on anyone medically unfit, in which case it's best to hire some help (if you can't find volunteers) to do the manhandling.

Even if you're fit, don't treat building a rock garden or a stone wall as a weight-lifting exercise. There's no need to lift and carry rocks – it's better to use the principle of leverage whenever possible. A strong sack trolley is ideal for moving small or medium-sized rocks around the garden, though you'll need to lay down strong planks over the lawn or soft earth.

Heavy rocks can also be moved over rollers if manipulated onto a strong board first. Old iron pipes or short lengths of scaffolding poles, or even old wooden broom handles, will do. As you roll the rock forward, move each roller from the back as it is released, and place it at the front. Once into a rhythm this is not as tedious as it sounds.

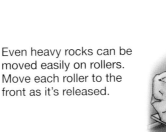

Take special care when moving rocks up a slope. This is one way to do it, though for a large rock you may need a couple of people at each end.

Even heavy rocks can be moved easily on rollers. Move each roller to the front as it's released.

Slopes pose a special problem. Try securing the rock with strong rope and pulling it up along a plank while helpers steady it and take the strain (see above). If that doesn't move it safely, hire some help. Mechanical equipment will make short work of something that could otherwise take considerable time and effort.

Once your rock is in about the right position, most of the fine tuning and positioning can be done by levering it with a crowbar or strong pole. If necessary, use a piece of wood or another stone as a fulcrum.

71

Centres of attraction

You don't actually have to make something with your rocks, simply letting them be there to speak for themselves may be enough. Don't overlook rocks as potential garden ornaments!

Rocks can make stunning focal points, in much the same way as an expensive carved ornament. Just choose an appropriate rock (or group of them) and position carefully. Provided you meet these two criteria you should have a focal point that will add immeasurably to a strong sense of garden design.

A large rock will make a strong feature in a large garden, and may even dominate a small one, but it should always look in proportion to its surroundings. However, the size of the rock is less important than where it's placed and how well it looks in a particular setting.

A group of strategically placed attractive beach pebbles in a gravel garden may serve a similar function to a large upright angular block of

Fixing

Large pebbles and rounded rocks may not require special fixing, though for stability, and to ensure they are not easily moved around, it's worth sinking the base of each one in a slight depression in the ground.

Large rocks, especially those that are tall and narrow or not naturally stable, are best mortared into position. Don't do this immediately, but wait until you've viewed the rock from many different angles to be sure the position is exactly right.

Mortar these large rocks to a concrete footing just below the surrounding ground level. You can always mask the base with plants.

granite in a rolling green lawn. If you're setting your rock or rocks among plants, they need to be large to stand out from their backdrop.

Choosing your rock

There's no satisfactory alternative to looking at lots of rocks, perhaps at a local quarry or a good stone merchant, and selecting an appropriate piece.

You should also consider the characteristics of the local landscape. A large chunk of angular granite may look pleasing in parts of the country where this rock is found, but rather harsh and inappropriate elsewhere. In a sandstone area, smoother, more rounded rocks may look better. But choosing an ornamental rock is a personal thing, like choosing a painting or an sculpture — in the final analysis you should choose what pleases you and expresses your artistic taste.

In this situation the single large rock would have looked incongruous, but by forming part of a group of rocks it becomes an interesting focal point.

Rock and water

Water and rock are good companions, and by adding moving water to a rock that's already a focal point you'll significantly enhance its impact.

You can buy drilled boulders from specialist suppliers, and all you need is a sunken, hidden reservoir and a small submerged pump. If you choose your rock first, you may have to ask a stone merchant to drill it for you. If possible, have a metal tube inserted to which you can fix a hose at the base.

Small drilled boulders can be supported on reservoirs sold for pebble fountains that come complete with a 'lid' to support the weight of your feature rock. These may be inadequate for the weight of a large rock, and a more substantial hidden support may be necessary. A strong steel mesh can be supported above the reservoir, then hidden with beach pebbles.

Maintenance

Top up the reservoir regularly in dry weather. Water will always be lost through evaporation, and sometimes through wind-blown splashes, and your submersible pump will be damaged if the water level drops to the point at which it is exposed. It's a good idea to leave a small space for a dipstick with the minimum acceptable level marked, which you can keep nearby.

Pumps occasionally need cleaning or servicing. In time they may even require replacing. Bear access in mind when making your feature and choosing the size of rock — it may have to be moved.

A rock will look that much more interesting with water to enhance the qualities of its surface.

Stepping stones

Stepping stones across water invite you to cross and explore. You can create a similar irresistible attraction across a lawn or along a path if you lead with a trail of interesting stones to step on.

You'll need a supply of suitably flat stones, and those sold for paving are ideal if you're setting them fairly flush into grass or perhaps along the centre of a gravel path. If your stepping stones are mainly a decorative device, perhaps to lead the eye across a lawn to another interesting view of the garden — even though it's not intended that you should use them as a path — it may be more important that the stones are decorative; whether they have a flush surface will be less relevant in this case.

Along a path

It may seem a waste to insert stepping stones along a path, yet it can transform a potentially boring one into a path packed with character and interest. Once you have stones to step on, the path invites exploration.

Setting the stones flush with the path makes walking easier but is more bland as a design element. Raising them above the surrounding path slows progress but means you have to pick your way along the path, just as you would across water. This not only looks interesting, it makes garden exploration for the visitor that much more fun. However, it's not a good option for a path that has to be used regularly, so reserve this use of stepping stones for feature paths.

Across a lawn

If your stepping-stone is to be a regular route across the lawn, sink the stones so that they are level with or just below the surrounding grass. If you want them primarily as a feature for occasional use, raising the top above the surrounding lawn will make your path more fun to use.

Strewing stones

If you have a few small stones or beach pebbles left over from another project, you could try scattering them in a purposeful way to bring interest to a dull corner. Projects don't come any easier than this!

While a heap of stones might resemble an ancient burial mound or a cairn rather more than a garden decoration, the clever use of strewn stones can work well for dull or difficult areas in need of something a little different to liven them up.

Beach pebbles are especially useful for this, being both small and generally light in colour. Try using them at the edge of a pond that borders a flower bed, taking them from beneath the water level up into the bed and as a low drift among the plants.

Alternatively, you could try using them at the edge of a gravel path — perhaps in a gloomy area bounded by trees or large shrubs, where you could allow the pebbles to drift into and around the shrubs.

Above left: *Stepping stones are easy to lay, yet they can transform a path into a feature full of charm and character.*

Left: *These broken flintstones help to soften the effect of the surrounding concrete at the edge of a water feature. Their irregular shapes, and the contrasting colours where the flints have been broken, add a sculptural element.*

75

Useful information

You'll find all kinds of useful facts and explanations on the next four pages. They should help you to understand some of those unfamiliar terms, and get to grips with things like the best concrete or mortar mixes for particular jobs.

Aggregate
Sand or gravel (small stones) that is mixed with cement to form concrete. Sand is sometimes described as *fine aggregate*, and stones or gravel as *coarse aggregate*.

Coarse aggregate can be either gravel or crushed stone, varying in size from 0.3 in (5 mm) to 0.75 in (20 mm). If you are laying concrete less than 2 in (5 cm) thick, choose an aggregate not more than 0.4 in (10 mm) in size.

See also **ballast**.

Ballast
A mix of sand and gravel, used in making concrete. The terms *all-in ballast* and *combined aggregate* are sometimes used for this.

See also **aggregate**.

Batter
The slope or taper of a face of a wall. A batter gauge is an improvised wooden frame with one or both sides fixed at an angle, used as a guide to check a consistent slope to a wall, especially dry stone walls which depend on their shape for much of their stability. See page 36.

Bolster chisel see **cold chisel**.

Bond
The way bricks or blocks are staggered to spread the load along a wall, or to interlock for a path.

Bricklayer's line
A length of string (usually nylon string) stretched between pegs or blocks that acts as a guide to ensure that stones are horizontal when each course is being laid.

Builder's square
A wooden device (usually improvised and made at home) for ensuring that corners are at right-angles. A home-made wooden builder's square is described on page 9, but you can also buy one if you prefer.

Capping see **coping**.

Cavity wall
A two-skinned wall with a space in the middle, normally used in the construction of buildings to provide insulation and reduce the risk of

 Concrete mixes

Special concrete mixes are sometimes used for particular situations, but the following two formulae will cover the projects described in this book. They refer to parts by volume. It doesn't matter whether you use a bucket, a wheelbarrow or a shovel, provided you keep to the same measure for each ingredient.

1 For foundations and footings, such as the base for a masonry wall:
   - one part Portland cement
   - two-and-a-half parts sharp sand
   - three-and-a-half parts aggregate.

   Instead of separate sand and aggregate, you can use five parts of ballast.

2 As a base for paving or patio:
   - one part Portland cement
   - two parts sharp sand
   - three parts aggregate.

   Instead of separate sand and aggregate, you can use four parts of ballast.

lamp inside walls. Garden walls are sometimes built with a large cavity that can be filled with soil for planting.

Cement

This is the hardening agent used for concrete and mortar. The kind usually available at large DIY stores and builders' merchants is *Portland cement* (a type, not a brand). It's usually grey in colour, though additives can be used to change the colour.

You can use additives when mixing concrete or mortar to make it more waterproof.

Masonry cement, used for mortar, already has a plasticiser added (see **plasticiser**).

Cold chisel

A tool with a broad cutting edge that distributes the energy of a hammer blow along a wide line. It is used to chip away stone, or to split stone along a line.

A **bolster chisel** has a wide blade, making it more useful for splitting rocks.

Club hammer

A heavy hammer used for jobs such as hitting a cold chisel or bolster chisel (these are used for splitting stone slabs, for example).

Combined aggregate see **ballast**.

Coping

The top course of a brick, block or stone wall, usually designed with an overlap to throw some of the rainwater clear of the wall. Coping is designed to prevent moisture seeping into the exposed joints on the top of the wall. Coping slabs are usually made from concrete, but large flat stones are usually used for a stone wall.

The term is used loosely to cover both *true coping* (which has an overlap) and *capping*, which is the correct term for when the coping is flush with the wall.

Course

An individual horizontal row of bricks or stones.

Crowbar

A long metal rod with a flat tip on one end and sometimes a claw on the other. The length of the bar makes it useful for levering and exerting pressure once the end has been wedged into position.

Float

A float trowel has a large, flat, rectangular blade and is used to level and smooth concrete. The blade is usually wooden. The similar steel tool is sometimes called a *plasterer's trowel*, but it can also be used for smoothing concrete or rendering mortared walls.

Footing

A concrete foundation or platform to provide a stable base for a wall.

Geologist's hammer

A hammer with a head shaped like a small pick-axe: one end flat, the other tapering to a point. Relatively light in weight, it's useful for shaping or chipping stone.

Goggles see **safety goggles**.

Hardcore

Broken bricks or stones, used to provide a sub-base for concrete footings or foundations.

Line blocks

Blocks that are placed at the corners of walls, attached to a line, and used to ensure that each course is laid level.

Mallet

Carpenters use a wooden mallet to drive wood chisels. Mallets with rubber/plastic heads can be used for tapping paving, bricks or blocks to level them.

Piers

Columns used to buttress and strengthen a wall. They are also useful at the end of a wall for hanging a gate.

Mixing mortar

The following formulae are recommended for mortar. As with the concrete mixtures on page 76, they are given here in parts per volume.

1   For bedding paving slabs, use a mortar of one part Portland cement to three parts soft sand.

2   For laying bricks and stones for walls, use one part Portland cement to six parts soft sand, with a plasticiser added.

It's often more convenient to use masonry cement, which already contains a plasticiser: one part masonry cement to five parts soft sand.

If a stronger mortar is required, such as for a very exposed position, reduce the sand to four parts and three parts respectively.

Planning permission

You may need planning permission from your local authority for a garden wall more than 6 ft 6 in (2 m) high, or 3 ft 3 in (1 m) if it's a boundary wall adjoining a highway. Consult your local authority for advice.

Plasticiser

This is usually used instead of the traditional lime to make a mortar mix that's easier to work with. The mortar is more aerated, reducing the risk of cracking if it's laid in cold weather. Masonry cement already has a plasticiser added.

Plumb-line

A weighted device attached to a cord, used to determine a true vertical. Gravity ensures that the cord hangs exactly vertical.

Safety goggles

Essential wear for anyone breaking or chipping stone, as they protect the eyes from any flying fragments. You can even buy types of goggles that are large enough to wear over the top of ordinary spectacles.

Sand

Everyone knows what sand is, but there are several types that are used in garden construction. *Sharp sand* (sometimes called *concreting sand*), which is coarse and gritty, should be used for concrete. *Soft sand* (sometimes called *builders' sand*), which is finer, is used for mortar.

Spirit-level

A tool with a flat surface and glass tubes or vials containing a bubble of air. When the bubble is centred, the structure is absolutely horizontal or vertical (depending on which way up the tool is used and which tube is relevant). For garden construction choose one 2–3 ft (60–90 cm) long.

Stone hammer

A heavy hammer, usually with one flat face and the other end bevelled and pointed, used to split and break rock.

Straight-edge

A long, perfectly straight piece of wood, used to support a spirit-level that itself is not long enough to span the area being checked.

Tamp

To bang down and consolidate (hardcore or sand, for example).

Trowel

There are various kinds of trowel used by builders. The three most common ones are the *bricklayer's trowel* used for handling and placing mortar (the blade has a flat surface, tapering to a point); the *pointing trowel*, which is similar but smaller; and the *float trowel*, which is used for smoothing concrete or a mortar render (see **float**).

This vertical stone makes an ideal focal point in the centre of a colourful flower bed.

Wall tie

A wire or wire-mesh device that can be mortared between bricks, walling blocks or stones at points of potential weakness, and to 'tie' two separate twin walls either side of a cavity together.

Wall ties are available from large DIY stores and builders' merchants.

Weep hole

A small gap left at intervals at the base of a raised bed or retaining wall, to allow moisture to seep away. See page 33.

Index

aggregate 76
angle-grinder 9

ballast 76
batter gauge 36, 76
block splitter 9
bolster chisel 8, 77
bond 76
boundary walls 30
bricklayer's line 76
builders' merchants 10
builder's square 9, 76
buying
    gravel 51
    liners 56
    rock and stone 10-14, 60
    tools 8-9

cap stones 31, 36
cascade 56-59
cavity wall 77
cement 77
centres of attraction 72, 79
chalk 12
circular raised beds 24-27
clothing 8
club hammer 8, 77
cold chisel 8, 77
concrete mixing 9, 76
coping 77
crazy-paving 16
crevice plants 21
crowbars 9, 37, 77
cutting stones 19, 28

dams 58
decking 54, 55
decorative steps 42, 47
dressed stone 14
dry stone walls 32, 34-38

edges 19, 22, 49
equipment 8-9

filling raised beds 27
flints (raised beds) 24, 25

float trowel 77
focal points 72, 79
footing 16, 25, 26, 30, 38, 77
footware 8
formal gravel gardens 48-51

garden centres 10
garden walls 28-37
geologist's hammer 77
gloves 8
goggles 8, 78
granite 12
gravel gardens 48-53

hammers 8, 9, 77, 78
hardcore 77
heavy stones 37, 71
hiring tools 9

informal gravel gardens 52
introduction 5
island rock beds 64

killing grass 49

lifting rocks 37, 71
limestone 12
line blocks 77
liners 56, 59, 69

mallet 77
materials 10-14, 60, 67
Mediterranean pond 66-69
miniature rock gardens 70
mortar 32, 78
mortared flints 25

natural angles 61

paths 16-22
paving stones
    buying 11
    laying 16-22
    raised beds 26
piers 77
planning permission 78
planting in walls 32, 41, 63
plants 6, 21, 33, 47, 53, 55
plasticiser 78
plumb-line 36, 78
pointing trowel 9
ponds 66-69

pumps 58, 68, 73

raised beds 24-27
raising heavy stones 37, 71
random stone 14
rectangular paving 20-22
removing bumps 19, 29
retaining walls 38-41
risers 43
rock beds 64
rock cascades 56-59
rock features 72
rock gardens 60-63, 70
rockery stone 12-13
rocks with water 56-59, 73

safety measures 62, 71
sand 78
sandstone 12
shaping stones 19, 28-29
sink garden 70
slabs see paving stones
slate 13
spirit-level 9, 78
splitting stones 28-29
stepping stones 74
steps 42-47
stone gardens 54-55
stone hammer 9, 78
stones see materials
straight-edge 9, 78
strewing stones 74

timber decking 54, 55
tools 8-9
traditional rock garden 60-63
treads 43
trimming stones 19, 22
trowels 9, 77, 78
tufa 13

wall plants 32, 33
wall tie 79
walling stone 14
water features 56-59, 66-69, 73
water pump 58, 68, 73
weep holes 33, 39, 79

York stone paving 11